WORKING IN
TECHNOLOGY

by Lauren Boritzke

STORY LIBRARY

www.12StoryLibrary.com

12-Story Library is an imprint of Bookstaves and Press Room Editions

Produced for 12-Story Library by Red Line Editorial

Photographs ©: arsenik/iStockphoto, cover, 1; Everett Historical/Shutterstock Images, 4; Halfpoint/iStockphoto, 5; izusek/iStockphoto, 6; Karen Blakeman, 7; Kirby Photo/iStockphoto, 8; George Dolgikh/Shutterstock Images, 9; ESB Professional/Shutterstock Images, 10; rzelich/iStockphoto, 11; Twin Design/Shutterstock Images, 12; Eva Katalin/iStockphoto, 13; humonia/iStockphoto, 14; shapecharge/iStockphoto, 15; Federico Rostagno/Shutterstock Images, 16, 29; scanrail/iStockphoto, 17; sfam_photo/Shutterstock Images, 18; FatCamera/iStockphoto, 19; Jonathan Weiss/Shutterstock Images, 20; Joseph Sohm/Shutterstock Images, 21; julief514/iStockphoto, 22, 28; asiseeit/iStockphoto, 23; Sky Nesher/iStockphoto, 24; Benny Marty/Shutterstock Images, 25; Kevin Krejci CC2.0, 26; David Berkowitz CC2.0, 27

Library of Congress Cataloging-in-Publication Data
Names: Boritzke, Lauren, author.
Title: Working in technology / by Lauren Boritzke.
Description: Mankato, MN : 12 Story Library, [2018] | Series: Career files | Includes bibliographical references and index.
Identifiers: LCCN 2016047449 (print) | LCCN 2016054183 (ebook) | ISBN 9781632354501 (hardcover : alk. paper) | ISBN 9781632355171 (pbk. : alk. paper) | ISBN 9781621435693 (hosted e-book)
Subjects: LCSH: Information technology--Vocational guidance--Juvenile literature. | Computer science--Vocational guidance--Juvenile literature.
Classification: LCC T58.5 .B6474 2018 (print) | LCC T58.5 (ebook) | DDC 004.023--dc23
LC record available at https://lccn.loc.gov/2016047449

Printed in the United States of America
022017

Access free, up-to-date content on this topic plus a full digital version of this book. Scan the QR code on page 31 or use your school's login at 12StoryLibrary.com.

Table of Contents

Computer Technology Picks Up the Pace

The world was a much slower place before computer technology. The first computers were built in the late 1930s and early 1940s. They were expensive machines the size of whole rooms. By the 1980s, cheaper and smaller personal computers became available for home use. And in the 1990s, the Internet made computers valuable tools for communication. Computers have continued to become more portable and more useful. Today, millions of people around the world use smartphones. These devices have far more computing power than the original room-sized computers.

Electronic innovations of all kinds have connected people around the

Social Security Administration clerks in the 1940s used giant machines to tabulate results.

world. They have inspired inventions and created millions of jobs. Technology's role in daily life continues to grow. Some jobs once performed by humans are now completed by computers or machines. But technology also creates new jobs by changing the way humans work.

There are many ways to prepare for a career in computer technology. Helping family or friends on the computer can be good practice. A career in technology is a way to help people by solving problems. It requires creativity. However, it is a new frontier. Pursuing a career in technology means preparing for jobs that may not even exist yet.

Today, computers are small enough to take them anywhere.

THINK ABOUT IT

Apple released its first portable computer in 1989. The computer cost $6,500. It weighed 16 pounds (7.3 kg). In what ways have technology companies improved on portable computer devices since 1989?

87

Percentage of US teenagers, ages 13 to 17, who have access to a computer.

- Technology has connected people around the world and made new inventions possible.
- A career in technology allows workers to help people, be creative, and solve problems.
- Career opportunities in technology are changing rapidly.

2

What Skills Are Needed to Work in Technology?

Many different interests may point to a future career in technology. For example, people who like to play video games have an interest in following steps to fix a problem. This is an important skill in computer programming. People who enjoy art might be interested in web design.

Society depends on technology in many ways. It's an exciting, constantly changing industry. It also

Many people who work in technology also work with other people, so it's important to have good communication skills.

requires a lot of problem solving and patience. Programmers and specialists need to keep working on problems until they are fixed. Questions such as "How does that work, and why?" or "How can a task be done better or faster?" should be asked every day in technology jobs.

Computer technology requires a lot of specialized knowledge. But it is important to start with the basics. Students interested in this field can focus on coding, science, math, or design. These subjects are good starting points for a variety of computer careers.

55,367
Number of US students who graduated with a bachelor's degree in computer science in the 2014–15 school year.

- A career in technology requires both logical and creative skills.
- Problem solving is an important part of many technology jobs.
- Coding, science, math, and design are all important subjects to study for a future career in technology.

Technicians take computers apart and have to be able to put them back together.

3

Coding Is Technology's Best Friend

Every career requires special skills. Musicians play perfect scales. Doctors know the name of every bone in the body. In technology, coding is one key to success.

Many schools and businesses are now teaching coding to their students and employees.

People who write code give instructions to computers in a way

```
 isIdentityAssertion) {
ing passwordWant = null;
  {
    passwordWant = database.getUserPassword(userName);
  catch (NotFoundException shouldNotHappen) {}
    String passwordHave = getPasswordHave(userName, callbacks);
  if (passwordWant == null || !passwordWant.equals(passwordHave
      throwFailedLoginException(
        "Authentication Failed: User " + use
        "Have " + passwordHave + ". Wan
      );
  }
}
} else {
  // anonymous login - let it through?
  System.out.println("\tempty userName");
}
log.  eeded = true;
principalsForSubject.add(new WLSUserImpl(user
addGroupsForSubject(userName);
    oginSucceeded;
```

Many programmers use if-then statements, which instruct the computer to perform a task only if certain conditions are met.

11 million

Number of professional programmers in the world.

- Programmers use code to tell computers what to do.
- Code is written in a specific order and format.
- Many different coding languages are currently in use.

THINK ABOUT IT

There are many different coding languages in use. Why do you think some coding languages become more popular than others?

the computers can understand. Each instruction communicates a task, such as "type the letter *A*" or "send an e-mail." Code must be written in a specific order and format. If something is out of place, the program will not work correctly.

There are many different coding languages to choose from. Java, C++, C#, and Python are just a few of the most common examples. Each uses its own particular wording and formatting. Each is suited to a different type of project. Some are easier or more difficult to learn.

There is code behind all sorts of everyday items. Phones, websites,

Most applications for Android devices use Java coding.

televisions, and computers all require code. Programmers write this code. Classes and online programs make coding easier to learn. Some websites even offer free classes online.

4

Computer Programmers Tell Computers What to Do

Learning to write code opens up many opportunities in technology. Computer programmers use code on a daily basis. Programmers use code to tell a computer what to do.

There are many different types of coding for programmers to choose from. Some coders build interactive websites. Others create programs for personal computers. And some develop video games. Some programmers work alone on small projects. Others work in teams. Big projects can take months or years to complete.

At the start of a project, a software developer shares how he or she wants the software to work. Programmers turn the developer's vision into a language the computer can understand. After they write the code, they test their work.

Computer programmers sometimes have to work long hours.

MAKING GAMES

Video game programmers work in a highly creative technology career. But there are other important jobs involved in making video games, too. Artists work on the visual aspects of the game. This can include scenery and characters. Level editors create the layout of the game's environments. And QA testers find any flaws in the game. These need to be fixed before the game becomes available to customers.

This requires patience. Sometimes things go wrong. Then the programmer must rewrite the code so the computer carries out its tasks correctly. Computer programming requires a mix of problem solving and creativity.

$79,530
Average annual salary for a computer programmer in the United States in 2015.

- Computer programmers translate the idea for a program into code.
- Programmers can work on websites, apps, video games, and more.
- Programmers test their programs and fix errors when they occur.

The continued popularity of Tetris proves that video games do not have to use complex coding to be successful.

Software Developers Come Up with Big Ideas

What do social media platforms, video games, and 3-D printing have in common? They were designed and invented by software developers. Software developers are the creative inventors of technology. Like any good inventor, software developers try to create products that will make life easier or more fun for others.

Developers design software that solves a problem. They want the software to be easy to use and understand. Developers need to know coding. However, they do not often use it. Developers create diagrams and charts. These help programmers write the code. Developers then troubleshoot problems. They return to the drawing board when software updates are needed. Many developers get started by developing their own programs for fun.

Mobile app development is one fast-growing area. In 2008, only 65,000 apps were available on the

Some software developers have to figure out how desktop applications should work on mobile devices.

People can use virtual reality to experience the thrills of riding a roller coaster without even leaving their homes.

Apple App Store. By 2016, there were more than 2 million apps to choose from. These apps offer ways to check the weather, shop, play games, and more. And all of this can be done from a smartphone or tablet. With each app, software developers aim to change the way humans interact with technology.

1,000
Average number of apps submitted to the Apple App Store every day.

- Software developers design mobile apps, computer programs, and web networks.
- Software developers come up with ideas for new programs.
- Software developers change the way humans interact with technology.

A WHOLE NEW WORLD

Virtual reality is a revolutionary area of software development. Digitally created environments appear realistic once users put on a headset that covers their eyes. A whole new world is projected for the user. Through this technology, users might find themselves hiking mountains or flying in spaceships. Virtual reality is used mainly for entertainment. However, the military and other industries have found practical uses for it as well.

Web Developers Create Websites

The Internet has touched the lives of billions of people over the past few decades. People can now shop, talk to friends, and take classes, all from a computer or mobile device. This has made the world seem a lot smaller.

None of this would be possible without web developers. They are the creative people who design and build the millions of websites on the Internet. Businesses hire web developers to help display their products or ideas online. Web developers must have great communication skills. This helps them build a website that meets all of a client's needs.

Creating a website involves two things: design and coding. Creating a website that is easy to use and understand is the key goal. Some developers design the look of a website. This includes color schemes and the overall layout of the site. Other developers use technologies such as HTML and CSS to create a website's core. HTML is specially formatted text that tells a web browser the content of a

Designers have to make sure websites are easy to navigate.

SMART THINGS, SMART WORLD

The Internet of Things is an emerging idea where ordinary objects become "smart." Sensors can be built into cars, refrigerators, and other objects. They can then send information to smartphones. This creates new ways for people to interact with these objects.

14
Percentage of web developers who were self-employed in 2014.

- Web developers design how a website looks and write code that makes it function.
- The goal is to make a website that is easy to use and understand.
- Web developers can work for a business or be self-employed.

website. CSS is text that tells the browser how that content should look. Websites can be built with premade templates or completely from scratch.

An understanding of software and design is important for a web development career. Depending on a business's needs, a web developer may work full time or part time. Many web developers are self-employed. Businesses hire them as freelancers to build websites that are both beautiful and useful.

Developers test their designs with many people.

15

IT Workers Keep the System Running

Schools, businesses, and other places of work use technology to store data. Information technology (IT) workers keep track of how they do this. Their role is important in preventing network problems. They update software and equipment.

Servers play a part in the daily responsibilities of an IT worker. Servers are computers that help distribute information over networks, including the Internet. IT workers use security software to protect servers from cyberattacks.

IT workers are sometimes called to repair servers.

Data centers employ IT workers to keep client data secure.

Required skills for IT jobs are always changing. IT workers should be knowledgeable about coding, programming, and software.

IT workers also need good communication and leadership skills. This will help them manage the technology of an organization.

53,700
Number of new IT positions expected in the United States between 2014 and 2024.

- Businesses, schools, and organizations hire IT workers to keep their technology up to date.
- IT workers keep servers safe from cyberattacks.
- Software and programming skills are the foundation of IT jobs.

OUT THERE, SOMEWHERE

Cloud computing allows people to store data and files on servers that they access over the Internet, rather than on a local computer. Google Drive is an example of online data storage through the cloud. People and businesses can connect to their information wherever and whenever.

17

Computer Systems Analysts Build Better Businesses

Information technology can be more complex than simple computer updates and keeping servers safe. Businesses want to use technology in smart ways. Modern technology can help them sell more products and improve their customer service. This is the job of computer systems analysts.

No matter the industry, a computer systems analyst advises businesses on which technology and software programs are smart to use. First, they must learn how a business uses technology. Maybe it wants to interact with more customers or store more information. The next step is research. This helps the

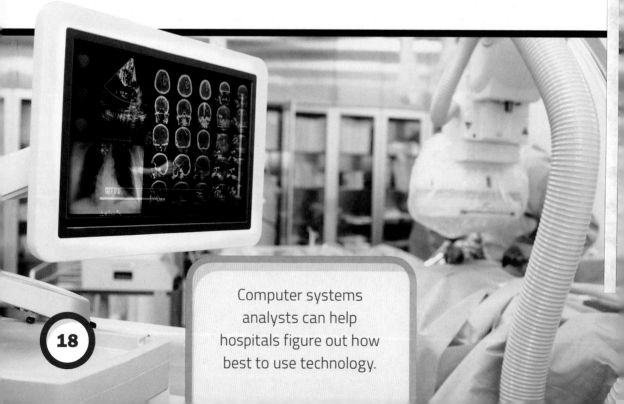

Computer systems analysts can help hospitals figure out how best to use technology.

computer systems analyst discover how to improve a business's practices. This job requires both IT and business knowledge.

An IT worker might install new software. But a computer systems analyst chooses that update. The analyst is responsible for training staff and employees on how to use it. This requires personalizing the new software to a company's needs. Outgoing problem solvers will thrive in this role. Computer systems analysts work with others constantly during their day. They will also benefit from confident decision-making skills.

$85,800

Average salary for a computer systems analyst in the United States in 2015.

- Computer systems analysts decide what technology businesses should use.
- Modern technology helps businesses sell more products and improve customer service.
- Computer systems analysts must be good at making decisions.

Universities and colleges use advice from computer systems analysts when planning computer labs.

Information Security Analysts Protect the Data

Many organizations store information that is not meant for the public. Classified government plans, medical records, and online banking files are all examples of private information. Information security analysts guard this data.

Information security analysts protect data from hackers. Hackers break into secure networks to get information.

Information security analysts create stronger security measures. Their job is to protect information.

This career involves a lot of troubleshooting and testing. Monitoring safety requires an understanding of how computers and software work. Information security analysts must fix

Health insurance company Anthem was hacked in 2015, affecting the personal data of more than 80 million people.

In 2016, hackers gained access to the e-mail account of John Podesta, the chairperson of Hillary Clinton's presidential campaign.

problems and block malware threats. They establish information recovery plans. They also train employees on these protection methods.

Information security analysts must be comfortable leading teams. They make difficult decisions. Protecting information in a digital age is a growing industry. Information security analysts are in high demand.

THINK ABOUT IT

By 2024, the field of information security is expected to grow much faster than the average rate for most fields. Why do you think that might be the case?

39

Percentage of all information breaches in 2015 that were in the health-care industry.

- Information security analysts protect digital data and networks from hackers.
- Troubleshooting, testing, and installing new security measures are common activities in this career.
- Information security analysts need strong leadership skills.

Computer Support Specialists Offer Assistance

Technology changes rapidly. This means users must regularly learn new skills. But sometimes this creates challenges. Computer support specialists help people around the world with their technology questions.

Computer support specialists help users solve problems on their computers or mobile devices. They use e-mail messages, phone calls, and online chats to connect with users. Sometimes issues cannot be fixed easily over the phone or Internet. Then support specialists perform in-person service calls at a business or home. This is common when a machine or computer is physically broken.

Computer support specialists ask customers to describe their computer problems.

Customer service skills are essential for this job. It is important to correct issues in a timely and friendly manner. Support specialists work in a variety of settings. They might work in universities, offices, or call centers. No matter where they are, support specialists are always a call or a click away, ready to help.

88,800
Estimated number of new jobs in computer support between 2014 and 2024.

- Computer support specialists solve Internet, software, and network problems for people around the world.
- These specialists respond to questions through e-mail, phone calls, or online chats.
- Computer support specialists need to have great customer service skills.

Some computer support specialists work at universities, showing students how to connect their mobile devices.

How to Get Started in a Technology Career

If a career in technology sounds like the right path, there are important steps to take to prepare for the future. There are many different education tracks toward a career in technology. Students can start by choosing classes in electronics, math, science, and computers. Some schools now include coding in their curriculum. Some free resources to learn coding can also be found online.

Most computer science jobs require a bachelor's degree. This is a four-year program at a college or university. Many students who plan to work in technology major in areas such as computer science, business, or data processing. However, there

Learning to use common computer applications helps students prepare for technology careers.

Google accepts approximately 1,500 interns out of 40,000 applicants each year.

is not one correct major for working with computers. Some jobs are also available to candidates with a two-year associate's degree.

40
Percentage of US schools that teach computer programming.

- Before college, students can take related high school classes.
- Most computer science jobs require a bachelor's degree.
- Internships display skills and experience to future employers.

Some technology careers, such as computer systems analysts and information security analysts, benefit from specialized knowledge and advanced degrees. These professionals may attend graduate school to earn a master's degree or even a doctorate.

Internships and fellowships are great experiences for young entry-level candidates. These opportunities help job seekers prove their interest and skills to future employers. Employers look not just for talent, but also for passion about technology.

25

The Future Changes with Technology

The future of technology is tightly connected to the capability of the Internet. The Internet will continue to change along with new devices, hardware, and software. Televisions and phones were invented long before the Internet came along. But today, inventors have adapted them to stream online videos and music. New technologies, such as virtual reality, are expected to push the boundaries of modern computers.

Changing technology will affect the way humans interact with their environment. However, innovation of new devices is a long process. In most cases, new technologies do not reach the public for years after they are invented. It takes time to make the hardware and test it. In contrast, developing a new mobile app can take only weeks.

The world has already felt the impact of technology. Objects such as refrigerators and self-driving cars can now

Robot for Tomorrow's Service Industry and Homes

Communication Android

Toshiba debuted a communication android at the 2015 Consumer Electronics Show.

65

Estimated percentage of children beginning elementary school who will work in careers that do not currently exist.

- Technology will revolutionize the future.
- New programs and technology require research, development, and testing.
- Virtual reality and smart objects are expected to change how humans work and learn.

HUMAN OR MACHINE

Scientists have been studying and developing the idea of artificial intelligence since the 1950s. It is the idea that a machine can be programmed to make intelligent decisions on its own. Some people are nervous about the idea of machines that can learn. But others see it as an exciting new opportunity.

connect to the Internet. Machines are changing how humans work in industries such as engineering and the military. Research and development on artificial intelligence and robotics could create new ways to learn and work. The number of opportunities for students in technology is exciting.

This fork collects data on a person's eating habits and then transmits the data to a website or app.

HAPILABS

HAPIfork
Eat Slowly - Lose Weight - Feel Great

The World's First Fork that Helps You Lose Weight

27

Other Jobs to Consider

Computer Research Scientist

Description: Study in-depth computing problems and work on solutions

Training/Education: Doctorate degree in computer science or a related field

Outlook: Growing

Average salary: $110,620

Computer Network Architect

Description: Plan and build computer networks

Training/Education: Bachelor's degree in computer science, engineering, or another related field

Outlook: Growing

Average salary: $100,240

Multimedia Artist and Animator

Description: Design computer graphics and animation for a variety of businesses, music videos, commercials, or events
Training/Education: Bachelor's degree in computer graphics, art, or a related field
Outlook: Steady
Average salary: $63,970

Computer, ATM, and Office Machine Repairer

Description: Repair and maintain performance of office technology
Training/Education: No formal education needed
Outlook: In decline
Average salary: $20.12/hour

Glossary

cloud computing
A system in which many small networks are connected through the Internet to allow large-scale data sharing.

data
Information collected in one place to be used for some purpose.

hardware
Computer equipment, such as a printer, monitor, or mobile device.

information technology
The use of computers to store, share, and organize information.

innovation
An invention or a new idea.

malware
Programs installed on a computer with the intent to cause damage.

server
A computer used to provide shared files to other computers in a network.

software
Programs installed on a computer that carry out certain tasks.

technology
Using science and engineering to fix a problem or make a task easier.

troubleshoot
To locate a problem and fix it.

virtual
Something created by a computer but made to seem real.

For More Information

Books

Briggs, Jason R. *Python for Kids: A Playful Introduction to Programming*. San Francisco, CA: No Starch Press, 2013.

Hustad, Douglas. *Discover Robotics*. Minneapolis, MN: Lerner Publications, 2017.

McManus, Sean. *How to Code in 10 Easy Lessons: Learn How to Design and Code Your Very Own Computer Game*. Lake Forest, CA: Walter Foster Jr., 2015.

Visit 12StoryLibrary.com

Scan the code or use your school's login at **12StoryLibrary.com** for recent updates about this topic and a full digital version of this book. Enjoy free access to:

- Digital ebook
- Breaking news updates
- Live content feeds
- Videos, interactive maps, and graphics
- Additional web resources

Note to educators: Visit 12StoryLibrary.com/register to sign up for free premium website access. Enjoy live content plus a full digital version of every 12-Story Library book you own for every student at your school.

Index

About the Author

Lauren Boritzke is a writer and freelance editor based in Minneapolis, Minnesota. She has worn many different hats in the book publishing industry, from intern to community outreach coordinator, and is the cofounder of *Daughter Lit Mag*.

READ MORE FROM 12-STORY LIBRARY

Every 12-Story Library book is available in many formats. For more information, visit 12StoryLibrary.com.